The Ultimate Travel Planner Workbook

Kristen D. Smith

ISBN-13: 978-1484956861
ISBN-10: 1484956869

Table of Contents

Finished with your long vacation? Get extra use out of this workbook by using it for your next two short vacations.

Travel Location:

Dates:

Where Can I Stay?

Where Can I Shop?

What Can I See?

What Do My Friends Say?

Miscellaneous Ideas:

Travel Location:

Dates:

What do I want or require in my lodgings?

Hotel Comparisons:

Bed and Breakfast Comparisons:

VRBO/etc. Comparisons:

Quick Tip: Hotels aren't always the nicest or cheapest places to stay for your money. If you've never tried a bed and breakfast, you're missing out! You can usually find B&B rooms for the same amount as a hotel, with added benefits of ambiance and a hot, home cooked breakfast. Other options, such as condos or cottages, give you added space and creature comforts of home. Check out websites such as www.bedandbreakfast.com or www.vrbo.com.

Travel Location:

Dates:

Price Shopping for Flights:

Price Shopping for Gasoline

Price Shopping for Auto Rentals:

Quick Tip: If you're planning on driving to your destination or renting a car once you've arrived, check out online resources such as gasbuddy.com and gaspricewatch.com to make sure that you find the lowest priced gasoline on your route. If you're doing a lot of driving, taking an extra few cents off per gallon could add up to the admission fare for another attraction!

Travel Location:

Dates:

Activities in the Area:

Travel Location:

Dates:

Notes:

Detailed Budget Planner

Expense	Planned Budget	Actual Budget
Hotels		
Bed and Breakfasts		
Cabins, Condos, and Cottages		
Camping Fees		
Airfare (Adults)		
Airfare (Children)		
Auto Rental		
Public Transit & Cab-fare		
Gasoline		
Parking		
Breakfast		
Lunch		
Dinner		
Snacks		
Groceries		
Alcohol		
Luggage		
Maps		
New Clothing		
Books & Magazines		
Souvenirs		
Gifts		
Medical Insurance		
Auto Insurance		
Personal Items Insurance		
Cancellation Insurance		
Other:		
Other:		
Other:		
Total Trip Cost		

Personalized Budget Planner

Expense	Planned Budget	Actual Budget
Total Trip Cost		

Mix and Match Wardrobe Designer:

Tops		Bottoms	
A	F	1	6
B	G	2	7
C	H	3	8
D	I	4	9
E	J	5	10

Write or Draw Your Clothing Choices to Plan Your Luggage

Shoes and Accessories		Planner			
		Day	Top	Bottom	Other
a	g				
b	h				
c	i				
d	j				
e	k				
f	l				

Daily Outfit Planner

Day One

What to Wear:

What to Pack:

Weather Report:

Day Two

What to Wear:

What to Pack:

Weather Report:

Day Three

What to Wear:

What to Pack:

Weather Report:

Daily Outfit Planner

Day Four

What to Wear:

What to Pack:

Weather Report:

Day Five

What to Wear:

What to Pack:

Weather Report:

Day Six

What to Wear:

What to Pack:

Weather Report:

Daily Outfit Planner

Day Seven

What to Wear: What to Pack:

Weather Report:

Day Eight

What to Wear: What to Pack:

Weather Report:

Day Nine

What to Wear: What to Pack:

Weather Report:

Daily Outfit Planner

Day Ten

What to Wear:

What to Pack:

Weather Report:

Day Eleven

What to Wear:

What to Pack:

Weather Report:

Day Twelve

What to Wear:

What to Pack:

Weather Report:

Our Trip Information

Travel Dates: _____

Lodging #1

Name: _____
Address: _____
Phone Number: _____
Directions: _____
Confirmation #: _____
Miscellany: _____

Lodging #2

Name: _____
Address: _____
Phone Number: _____
Directions: _____
Confirmation #: _____
Miscellany: _____

Flight #1

Airline: _____
Location: _____
Phone Number: _____
Flight Number: _____   Reference Number: _____
Check In Time: _____   Departure Time: _____
Boarding Info: _____   Arrival Time: _____
Miscellany: _____

Flight #2

Airline: _____
Location: _____
Phone Number: _____
Flight Number: _____   Reference Number: _____
Check In Time: _____   Departure Time: _____
Boarding Info: _____   Arrival Time: _____
Miscellany: _____

Auto Rental

Rental Company: _____
Address: _____
Phone Number: _____
Confirmation # _____   Miscellany: _____

Sight Seeing Information

Sight #1

Name: _____

Address: _____

Phone Number: _____

Directions: _____

Opening/Closing: _____

Cost per person: _____

Miscellany: _____

Sight #2

Name: _____

Address: _____

Phone Number: _____

Directions: _____

Opening/Closing: _____

Cost per person: _____

Miscellany: _____

Sight #3

Name: _____

Address: _____

Phone Number: _____

Directions: _____

Opening/Closing: _____

Cost per person: _____

Miscellany: _____

Sight #4

Name: _____

Address: _____

Phone Number: _____

Directions: _____

Opening/Closing: _____

Cost per person: _____

Miscellany: _____

Packing List

- [ ]
- [ ]
- [ ]
- [ ]
- [ ]
- [ ]
- [ ]
- [ ]
- [ ]
- [ ]
- [ ]
- [ ]
- [ ]
- [ ]
- [ ]
- [ ]
- [ ]
- [ ]
- [ ]
- [ ]
- [ ]
- [ ]
- [ ]
- [ ]
- [ ]
- [ ]
- [ ]
- [ ]

Packing List

☐   ☐

☐   ☐

☐   ☐

☐   ☐

☐   ☐

☐   ☐

☐   ☐

☐   ☐

☐   ☐

☐   ☐

☐   ☐

☐   ☐

☐   ☐

☐   ☐

☐   ☐

☐   ☐

☐   ☐

☐   ☐

☐   ☐

☐   ☐

☐   ☐

☐   ☐

☐   ☐

☐   ☐

☐   ☐

☐   ☐

☐   ☐

☐   ☐

Detailed Packing List

Clothing	Qty.	Toiletries
☐ Bras and Underwear		☐ Toothbrush
☐ Socks		☐ Toothpaste/Toothpowder
☐ Sleep wear and robe		☐ Mouthwash
☐ Jackets and Raincoats		☐ Dental Floss
☐ Coats		☐ Soap
☐ Sweaters and Sweatshirts		☐ Shampoo
☐ Umbrella		☐ Conditioner
☐ Hats		☐ Hair Spray
☐ Gloves		☐ Hair Products
☐ Scarves		☐ Deodorant
☐ Swimwear		☐ Moisturizer
☐ Casual Shirts		☐ Make up
☐ Dress shirts		☐ Make up remover
☐ Jeans		☐ Lip balm
☐ Shorts		☐ Sunscreen
☐ Slacks		☐ Insect Repellent
☐ Skirts		☐ Comb/Brush
☐ Dresses		☐ Shaving Cream
☐ Suits		☐ Shaving Razor
☐ Casual Shoes		☐ Nail Care Supplies
☐ Dress Shoes		☐ Contact Lenses/Solution
☐ Sandals/Flip Flops		☐ Birth Control Supplies
☐ Slippers		☐ Feminine Hygiene Products
☐ Ties		☐ Prescription Medications
☐ Belts		☐ Pain Reliever/OTC Medications
☐ Watch		☐ Vitamins
☐ Jewelry		☐ First Aid Kit
☐ Sunglasses		☐ Hand Sanitizer

Detailed Packing List, cont'd

Identification & Paperwork

- ☐ Passport
- ☐ Driver's License
- ☐ AAA/CAA Member Cards
- ☐ This book (itineraries, confirm. #s)
- ☐ Debit/Credit Cards
- ☐ Cash and Traveler's Cheques
- ☐ Photocopies of Passport and License
- ☐ Photocopies of Debit/Credit Cards
- ☐ Credit Card/Emergency Contact
- ☐ Medical Insurance Card
- ☐ Travel Insurance
- ☐ Phone Card/Useable cell phone
- ☐ Miscellaneous Tickets
- ☐ Maps and Guidebooks
- ☐

Miscellaneous

- ☐ Travel Pillow
- ☐ House Keys
- ☐ Books/Magazines
- ☐ Playing Cards/Board Games
- ☐ Notebook and Writing Utensils
- ☐ Snacks
- ☐ Children's Activities
- ☐ Laundry Bag
- ☐ Laundry Detergent
- ☐ Work Documents
- ☐
- ☐ _____
- ☐ _____
- ☐ _____
- ☐

Electronics

- ☐ Cell phone/Charger
- ☐ Laptop/Charger
- ☐ Camera/Charger
- ☐ Film/Memory Card
- ☐ Batteries
- ☐ Electrical converter/adaptor
- ☐ Music player/Headphones
- ☐ Ebook Reader
- ☐ Alarm Clock
- ☐
- ☐ _____
- ☐ _____

Babies and Young Children

- ☐ Formula and bottles
- ☐ Diapers and Diaper Bag
- ☐ Diaper Cream/Baby Powder
- ☐ Wet Wipes
- ☐ Child Carrier
- ☐ Stroller
- ☐ Pacifiers
- ☐ Baby Blanket
- ☐ Toys/Amusements
- ☐
- ☐ _____
- ☐ _____

Packing Tips

1. Rolling your clothes can not only make them smaller – thereby increasing the amount of clothing you can take with you – but it can also cut down on the amount of wrinkles you'll find when you unpack your bags. Fold back the sleeves or double up the pant legs and roll the fabric from the bottom up.

2. Store your toiletries in large, quart size plastic bags to keep them all together. You can put like items in smaller bags to place inside the larger one to prevent possible contaminations. Using plastic as a barrier also helps if you have anything liquid and prone to spillage! Keep in mind that TSA regulations only allow liquid containers of 3.4 oz by volume if you're catching a plane.

3. Be mindful of which valuables you decide to take with you. Stick to one or two pieces of jewelry that wouldn't cause you to be heartbroken if they were broken or stolen unless you plan to wear something that you never take off. Especially if you're traveling in a foreign country, tourists are prime targets for pickpockets and thieves – and it makes haggling with locals a bit more difficult if you're sporting some serious bling.

4. Using an e-reader can cut down on several pounds of books that you may otherwise take with you. Fill it up with all your favorites before you leave and don't forget to bring your charger! If you need a printed copy of a guidebook (ebooks can be hard to thumb through on the go) stick to one comprehensive book or two very slim volumes.

5. Don't pack items that are easy to buy at your destination – or if you do want to pack them, use smaller than original containers (a few pain relievers in a plastic baggie, sample size containers full of shampoo). Check airport regulations before you go so as to minimize any intrusive searches and discarding of your belongings at the checkpoints.

Daily Travel Planner

Date: _____

Site to Visit #1

Name:

Location:

Visitor Hours:

Admission Fee:

Notes:

Site to Visit #1

Name:

Location:

Visitor Hours:

Admission Fee:

Notes:

Site to Visit #1

Name:

Location:

Visitor Hours:

Admission Fee:

Notes:

Weather Report: What Can We Eat?

Timeline

7 a.m.

11 p.m.

Daily Travel Planner

Date: _____

Timeline

7 a.m.

Site to Visit #1

Name:

Location:

Visitor Hours:

Admission Fee:

Notes:

Site to Visit #1

Name:

Location:

Visitor Hours:

Admission Fee:

Notes:

Site to Visit #1

Name:

Location:

Visitor Hours:

Admission Fee:

Notes:

11 p.m.

Weather Report: What Can We Eat?

Daily Travel Planner

Date: _____

Site to Visit #1

Name:

Location:

Visitor Hours:

Admission Fee:

Notes:

Site to Visit #1

Name:

Location:

Visitor Hours:

Admission Fee:

Notes:

Site to Visit #1

Name:

Location:

Visitor Hours:

Admission Fee:

Notes:

Weather Report: What Can We Eat?

Timeline

7 a.m.

11 p.m.

Daily Travel Planner

Date: _____

Site to Visit #1

Name:

Location:

Visitor Hours:

Admission Fee:

Notes:

Site to Visit #1

Name:

Location:

Visitor Hours:

Admission Fee:

Notes:

Site to Visit #1

Name:

Location:

Visitor Hours:

Admission Fee:

Notes:

Weather Report: | What Can We Eat?

Timeline

7 a.m.

11 p.m.

Daily Travel Planner

Date: _____

Site to Visit #1

Name:

Location:

Visitor Hours:

Admission Fee:

Notes:

Site to Visit #1

Name:

Location:

Visitor Hours:

Admission Fee:

Notes:

Site to Visit #1

Name:

Location:

Visitor Hours:

Admission Fee:

Notes:

Weather Report: What Can We Eat?

Timeline

7 a.m.

11 p.m.

Daily Travel Planner

Date: _____

Site to Visit #1

Name:

Location:

Visitor Hours:

Admission Fee:

Notes:

Site to Visit #1

Name:

Location:

Visitor Hours:

Admission Fee:

Notes:

Site to Visit #1

Name:

Location:

Visitor Hours:

Admission Fee:

Notes:

Weather Report:

What Can We Eat?

Timeline

7 a.m.

11 p.m.

Daily Travel Planner

Date: _____

Timeline

7 a.m.

Site to Visit #1

Name:

Location:

Visitor Hours:

Admission Fee:

Notes:

Site to Visit #1

Name:

Location:

Visitor Hours:

Admission Fee:

Notes:

Site to Visit #1

Name:

Location:

Visitor Hours:

Admission Fee:

Notes:

Weather Report: What Can We Eat?

11 p.m.

Condensed Daily Planner

Day One	Sites to See	Grub to Eat	Reservations?	Notes
	☐			
	☐			
	☐			
	☐			

Day Two	Sites to See	Grub to Eat	Reservations?	Notes
	☐			
	☐			
	☐			
	☐			

Day Three	Sites to See	Grub to Eat	Reservations?	Notes
	☐			
	☐			
	☐			
	☐			

Day Four	Sites to See	Grub to Eat	Reservations?	Notes
	☐			
	☐			
	☐			
	☐			

Condensed Daily Planner

Day Five

Sites to See	Grub to Eat	Reservations?	Notes
☐			
☐			
☐			
☐			

Day Six

Sites to See	Grub to Eat	Reservations?	Notes
☐			
☐			
☐			
☐			

Day Seven

Sites to See	Grub to Eat	Reservations?	Notes
☐			
☐			
☐			
☐			

Day Eight

Sites to See	Grub to Eat	Reservations?	Notes
☐			
☐			
☐			
☐			

Condensed Daily Planner

Day Nine

Sites to See	Grub to Eat	Reservations?	Notes
☐			
☐			
☐			
☐			

Day Ten

Sites to See	Grub to Eat	Reservations?	Notes
☐			
☐			
☐			
☐			

Day Eleven

Sites to See	Grub to Eat	Reservations?	Notes
☐			
☐			
☐			
☐			

Day Twelve

Sites to See	Grub to Eat	Reservations?	Notes
☐			
☐			
☐			
☐			

Condensed Daily Planner

	Sites to See	Grub to Eat	Reservations?	Notes
Day Thirteen	☐ ☐ ☐ ☐			

	Sites to See	Grub to Eat	Reservations?	Notes
Day Fourteen	☐ ☐ ☐ ☐			

	Sites to See	Grub to Eat	Reservations?	Notes
Day Fifteen	☐ ☐ ☐ ☐			

	Sites to See	Grub to Eat	Reservations?	Notes
Day Sixteen	☐ ☐ ☐ ☐			

Travel Journal

Date and Location:

Travel Journal

Date and Location:

Travel Journal

Date and Location:

Travel Journal

Date and Location:

Travel Journal

Date and Location:

_____

Date and Location:

Travel Journal

Date and Location:

_____

Date and Location:

Travel Journal

Date and Location:

_____

Date and Location:

Travel Journal

Date and Location:

Date and Location:

Before We Leave...

- ☐ Pay outstanding or soon due bills
- ☐ Hold newspapers and/or mail
- ☐ Empty trash receptacles
- ☐ Empty refrigerator
- ☐ Lock doors and windows
- ☐ Unplug extraneous appliances
- ☐ Set thermostat
- ☐ Put lights/radio on timers
- ☐ Set Tivo to record your shows
- ☐ Leave house key with friend/neighbor
- ☐ Leave itinerary with friend/relative
- ☐ Arrange for a pet sitter
- ☐ Arrange for a house sitter/lawn care
- ☐ Check airline regulations for no-fly items
- ☐ Personalize your luggage and carry-ons
- ☐ Renew passport
- ☐ Transfer ebooks and music to devices
- ☐ Check baggage weights to avoid fees
- ☐ Arrange for disability accomodations
- ☐ Other: _____
- ☐ _____
- ☐ _____
- ☐ _____
- ☐ _____
- ☐ _____
- ☐ _____
- ☐ _____
- ☐ _____

While We're Gone

(Photocopy this page so that you can give it to anyone who needs it while you're away.)

We'll Be At:	Alarm Code:
Address:	Fire Department:
Phone One:	Police Department:
Phone Two:	The spare key is:
Miscellaneous:	Miscellaneous:
Airline Out:	Airline Home:
Flight Number:	Flight Number:
Departure Time:	Departure Time:
Arrival Time:	Arrival Time:
Miscellaneous:	Miscellaneous:
House Care Instructions:	Pet Care Instructions:

Notes:

Mini Trip #1

Travel Location:

Dates:

Where Can I Stay?

Where Can I Shop?

What Can I See?

What Do My Friends Say?

Miscellaneous Ideas:

Our Trip Information

Travel Dates: _____

Lodging #1

Name: _____
Address: _____
Phone Number: _____
Directions: _____
Confirmation #: _____
Miscellany: _____

Lodging #2

Name: _____
Address: _____
Phone Number: _____
Directions: _____
Confirmation #: _____
Miscellany: _____

Flight #1

Airline: _____
Location: _____
Phone Number: _____
Flight Number: _____ Reference Number: _____
Check In Time: _____ Departure Time: _____
Boarding Info: _____ Arrival Time: _____
Miscellany: _____

Flight #2

Airline: _____
Location: _____
Phone Number: _____
Flight Number: _____ Reference Number: _____
Check In Time: _____ Departure Time: _____
Boarding Info: _____ Arrival Time: _____
Miscellany: _____

Auto Rental

Rental Company: _____
Address: _____
Phone Number: _____
Confirmation # _____ Miscellany: _____

Sight Seeing Information

Sight #1

Name: _____

Address: _____

Phone Number: _____

Directions: _____

Opening/Closing: _____

Cost per person: _____

Miscellany: _____

Sight #2

Name: _____

Address: _____

Phone Number: _____

Directions: _____

Opening/Closing: _____

Cost per person: _____

Miscellany: _____

Sight #3

Name: _____

Address: _____

Phone Number: _____

Directions: _____

Opening/Closing: _____

Cost per person: _____

Miscellany: _____

Sight #4

Name: _____

Address: _____

Phone Number: _____

Directions: _____

Opening/Closing: _____

Cost per person: _____

Miscellany: _____

Packing List and Budget Considerations

Be Sure to Bring...		Expenses	Planned $	Actual $
☐				
☐				
☐				
☐				
☐				
☐				
☐				
☐				
☐				
☐				
☐				
☐				
☐				
☐				
☐				
☐				
☐				
☐				
☐				
☐				
☐				
☐				
☐				
☐				
☐				
☐				
☐				
		Total		

Daily Travel Planner

Date:_____

Site to Visit #1

Name:

Location:

Visitor Hours:

Admission Fee:

Notes:

Site to Visit #1

Name:

Location:

Visitor Hours:

Admission Fee:

Notes:

Site to Visit #1

Name:

Location:

Visitor Hours:

Admission Fee:

Notes:

Weather Report:

What Can We Eat?

Timeline

7 a.m.

11 p.m.

Daily Travel Planner

Date:_____

Site to Visit #1

Name:

Location:

Visitor Hours:

Admission Fee:

Notes:

Site to Visit #1

Name:

Location:

Visitor Hours:

Admission Fee:

Notes:

Site to Visit #1

Name:

Location:

Visitor Hours:

Admission Fee:

Notes:

Weather Report:

What Can We Eat?

Timeline

7 a.m.

11 p.m.

Daily Travel Planner

Date:_____

Timeline

7 a.m.

Site to Visit #1

Name:

Location:

Visitor Hours:

Admission Fee:

Notes:

Site to Visit #1

Name:

Location:

Visitor Hours:

Admission Fee:

Notes:

Site to Visit #1

Name:

Location:

Visitor Hours:

Admission Fee:

Notes:

Weather Report:

What Can We Eat?

11 p.m.

Travel Journal

Date and Location:

Travel Journal

Date and Location:

Travel Journal

Date and Location:

Mini Trip #2

Travel Location:

Dates:

Where Can I Stay?

Where Can I Shop?

What Can I See?

What Do My Friends Say?

Miscellaneous Ideas:

Our Trip Information

Travel Dates: _____

Lodging #1

Name: _____
Address: _____
Phone Number: _____
Directions: _____
Confirmation #: _____
Miscellany: _____

Lodging #2

Name: _____
Address: _____
Phone Number: _____
Directions: _____
Confirmation #: _____
Miscellany: _____

Flight #1

Airline: _____
Location: _____
Phone Number: _____
Flight Number: _____ Reference Number: _____
Check In Time: _____ Departure Time: _____
Boarding Info: _____ Arrival Time: _____
Miscellany: _____

Flight #2

Airline: _____
Location: _____
Phone Number: _____
Flight Number: _____ Reference Number: _____
Check In Time: _____ Departure Time: _____
Boarding Info: _____ Arrival Time: _____
Miscellany: _____

Auto Rental

Rental Company: _____
Address: _____
Phone Number: _____
Confirmation # _____ Miscellany: _____

Sight Seeing Information

Sight #1

Name: _____

Address: _____

Phone Number: _____

Directions: _____

Opening/Closing: _____

Cost per person: _____

Miscellany: _____

Sight #2

Name: _____

Address: _____

Phone Number: _____

Directions: _____

Opening/Closing: _____

Cost per person: _____

Miscellany: _____

Sight #3

Name: _____

Address: _____

Phone Number: _____

Directions: _____

Opening/Closing: _____

Cost per person: _____

Miscellany: _____

Sight #4

Name: _____

Address: _____

Phone Number: _____

Directions: _____

Opening/Closing: _____

Cost per person: _____

Miscellany: _____

Packing List and Budget Considerations

Be Sure to Bring...	Expenses	Planned $	Actual $
☐			
☐			
☐			
☐			
☐			
☐			
☐			
☐			
☐			
☐			
☐			
☐			
☐			
☐			
☐			
☐			
☐			
☐			
☐			
☐			
☐			
☐			
☐			
☐			
☐			
☐			
☐			
	Total		

Daily Travel Planner

Date:_____

Site to Visit #1

Name:

Location:

Visitor Hours:

Admission Fee:

Notes:

Site to Visit #1

Name:

Location:

Visitor Hours:

Admission Fee:

Notes:

Site to Visit #1

Name:

Location:

Visitor Hours:

Admission Fee:

Notes:

Weather Report: What Can We Eat?

Timeline

7 a.m.

11 p.m.

Daily Travel Planner

Date: _____

Site to Visit #1

Name:

Location:

Visitor Hours:

Admission Fee:

Notes:

Site to Visit #1

Name:

Location:

Visitor Hours:

Admission Fee:

Notes:

Site to Visit #1

Name:

Location:

Visitor Hours:

Admission Fee:

Notes:

Weather Report:

What Can We Eat?

Timeline

7 a.m.

11 p.m.

Daily Travel Planner

Date:_____

Site to Visit #1

Name:

Location:

Visitor Hours:

Admission Fee:

Notes:

Site to Visit #1

Name:

Location:

Visitor Hours:

Admission Fee:

Notes:

Site to Visit #1

Name:

Location:

Visitor Hours:

Admission Fee:

Notes:

Weather Report: What Can We Eat?

Timeline

7 a.m.

11 p.m.

Travel Journal

Date and Location:

Travel Journal

Date and Location:

Travel Journal

Date and Location:

10286952R00042

Printed in Great Britain
by Amazon.co.uk, Ltd.,
Marston Gate.